Level C · Book 2

QuickReads®
A Research-Based Fluency Program

Elfrieda H. Hiebert, Ph.D.

MODERN CURRICULUM PRESS

Pearson Learning Group

Program Reviewers and Consultants

Dr. Barbara A. Baird
Director of Federal Programs/Richardson ISD
Richardson, TX

Dr. Kate Kinsella
Dept. of Secondary Education and Step to College Program
San Francisco State University
San Francisco, CA

Pat Sears
Early Child Coordinator/Virginia Beach Public Schools
Virginia Beach, VA

Dr. Judith B. Smith
Supervisor of ESOL and World and Classical Languages/Baltimore City Public Schools
Baltimore, MD

The following people have contributed to the development of this product:

Art and Design: Adriano Farinella, Luis Ferreira, Dorothea Fox, Salita Mehta,
    Janice Noto-Helmers, Dan Thomas

Editorial: Lynn W. Kloss

Manufacturing: Michele Uhl

Marketing: Connie Buck

Production: Laura Benford-Sullivan, Jeffrey Engel

Publishing Operations: Jennifer Van Der Heide

1-800-321-3106
www.pearsonlearning.com

Contents

Contents

SCIENCE **The Solar System**

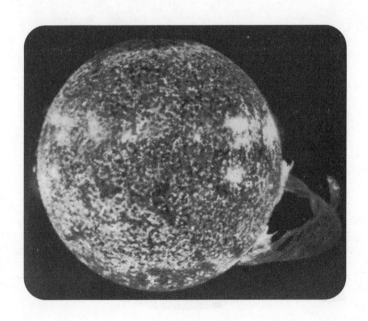

Contents

Rain Forests

Contents

Acknowledgments

All photographs © Pearson Learning unless otherwise noted.

Cover: © Frans Lanting/Minden Pictures.

3: Terry Renna/AP/Wide World Photos. 4: Katsumi 'Kasahara/AP/Wide World Photos. 5: NASA. 6: Patti Murphy/Animals Animals/Earth Scenes. 7: Michael Sewell/Peter Arnold, Inc. 8: Bob Daemmrich/Stock Boston, Inc/PictureQuest. 10: National Oceanic and Atmospheric Administration. 12: Luis M. Alvarez/AP/Wide World Photos. 14: Terry Renna/AP/Wide World Photos. 16: Michael Boys/Corbis. 18: Thomas S. England/TimePix. 24: Eric Draper/AP/Wide World Photos. 26: Roger RessMeyer/Corbis. 28: © Reuters/Corbis. 30: Katsumi 'Kasahara/AP/Wide World Photos. 38–42: NASA. Carlyn Iverson/Absolute Science. 46: Ken Hodges/NASA. 52: © Tom Van Sant/Photo Researchers, Inc. 52: Corbis. 56: L. Gould/Animals Animals/Earth Scenes. 58: Patti Murphy/Animals Animals/Earth Scenes. 60: Marc Epstein/DRK Photo. 66: © Gregory G. Dimijian/Photo Researchers, Inc. 68: Anup Shah/DRK Photo. 70: James P. Rowan/DRK Photo. 72: Michael Sewell/Peter Arnold, Inc. 74: SuperStock, Inc. 80: Richard Lord/PhotoEdit. 82: Bob Krist/Corbis. 84: Michael Newman/PhotoEdit. 86: Mark C. Burnett/Stock Boston, Inc/PictureQuest. 88: Bob Daemmrich/Stock Boston, Inc/PictureQuest.

Hurricanes

The circle is a hurricane forming over the sea.

What Is a Hurricane?

Hurricanes are storms that start at sea. As the Sun beats down on the sea, the water gets hot. The hot[25] water starts to evaporate. *Evaporate* means "to turn water into clouds."

As the clouds get big with evaporated water, the air around the clouds can[50] start to move very fast. When the winds are moving at 74 miles per hour or more, the storm is called a hurricane.

Many hurricanes[75] never reach land. Yet when a hurricane does reach land, the winds are so strong they can blow the roof off of a house. Hurricane[100] winds also can make big waves that cause floods.[109]

Hurricanes

Weather scientists track hurricanes to help people stay safe.

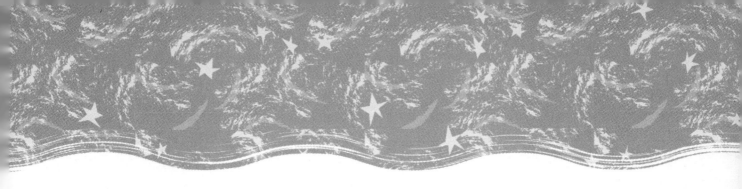

Tracking Hurricanes

People need to know when a hurricane is coming. Weather scientists help people by keeping track of hurricanes with computers. Using computers helps [25] weather scientists know when a hurricane has started out at sea. Computers can measure how fast the wind is blowing. Computers can also help people [50] know if the hurricane is moving toward land.

Hurricanes can last five to six days. Yet hurricanes do not stay over land for five to [75] six days. When a hurricane moves over land, the rain in the clouds starts to fall. The wind starts to slow down. Soon, the hurricane [100] is over. However, there can be lots to clean up after a hurricane. [113]

There can be lots to clean up after a hurricane.

Hurricane Cleanup

When a hurricane is over, parts of trees, houses, boats, and cars might be all over the ground. There might be no lights,[25] water, or food. Some people might have lost their homes or their cars. Some people might not be able to find their pets.

After a[50] strong hurricane, people often come from many places to help clean up. They tell people where it is safe to go. They look for people[75] and pets that are lost. They give water and food to people. Sometimes, homes have to be fixed or new homes have to be built.[100] The cleanup after a strong hurricane can take a long time.[111]

Hurricanes

Pets try to find a safe place to hide during hurricanes.

Pets in Hurricanes

When a strong hurricane is about to hit, people have to leave their homes quickly and go to shelters. They cannot take[25] their pets with them to shelters. Pets are left in their homes. Some pets run away because they are afraid. However, most pets do not[50] run very far. They often hide in places near their homes where they feel safe. When people come back home, they should look for their[75] pets near their homes and at pet shelters.

People should be sure that their pets wear tags that tell where they live. In that way,[100] if pets run away during a hurricane, people will find them quickly.[112]

Hurricane Andrew caused a lot of harm in the United States.

Hurricane Names

Giving hurricanes names helps people to keep track of hurricanes. Each year, 21 names are picked for hurricanes. The first hurricane in a year starts with the letter A.

If a girl's name is used for the first hurricane one year, the first hurricane of the next year will get a boy's name. In the year 2000, the first hurricane was called Alberto. In 2001, the first hurricane was named Allison.

The names of very big storms are used only once. The first hurricane in 1992, Hurricane Andrew, was a very big storm. It caused a great deal of harm. The name Andrew will never be used for a hurricane again.

Hurricanes

Write words that will help you remember what you learned.

What Is a Hurricane?

_____

_____

_____

_____

Tracking Hurricanes

_____

_____

_____

_____

Hurricane Cleanup

_____

_____

_____

_____

Pets in Hurricanes

_____

_____

_____

_____

Hurricane Names

_____

_____

_____

_____

What Is a Hurricane?

1. What is the main idea of "What Is a Hurricane?"

   Ⓐ Hurricanes start on land and move to the sea.

   Ⓑ Most hurricanes do not reach land.

   Ⓒ Hurricanes are big storms that start at sea.

   Ⓓ Hurricanes are big clouds.

2. How does a hurricane start?

_____

_____

_____

Tracking Hurricanes

1. How do people track hurricanes?

   Ⓐ by watching the rain that falls

   Ⓑ with radios

   Ⓒ by knowing when they will come to land

   Ⓓ with computers

2. What happens when a hurricane comes to land?

_____

_____

_____

Hurricane Cleanup

1. Another good name for "Hurricane Cleanup" is _____

Ⓐ "After a Hurricane."

Ⓑ "Before a Hurricane."

Ⓒ "Building New Towns."

Ⓓ "Big Hurricanes."

2. Why do people need help after a hurricane?

_____

_____

_____

Pets in Hurricanes

1. "Pets in Hurricanes" is MAINLY about _____

Ⓐ what happens to pets in hurricanes.

Ⓑ how pets find their way home after hurricanes.

Ⓒ how to put tags on pets.

Ⓓ why pets cannot go to shelters during hurricanes.

2. During hurricanes, what often happens to dogs and cats?

_____

_____

_____

Hurricane Names

1. What kind of names do hurricanes get?

Ⓐ the names of animals

Ⓑ the names of people who track them

Ⓒ first names

Ⓓ the names of other big hurricanes

2. How are hurricanes named each year?

_____

_____

_____

Connect Your Ideas

1. Do you think it is important to track hurricanes?
Why or why not?

_____

_____

_____

2. What would you do if you were in a place where a
hurricane might come?

_____

_____

_____

Earthquakes

Earthquakes can make buildings fall down.

Old Stories About Earthquakes

1. What is the main idea of "Old Stories About Earthquakes"?

   Ⓐ Earthquakes are caused by shaking rocks.

   Ⓑ People made up stories to explain earthquakes.

   Ⓒ The earth shakes because plates move.

   Ⓓ People told stories about fish and dogs.

2. Why did people ~~tell~~ told stories about earthquakes? ~~because~~ to explain

   So people can feel less afraid mad up stories about them. And huge catfish was moving its tail. People in Rusia said that the dog that pulled the world's like asled.

Connect Your Ideas

1. Describe two things you have learned about earthquakes.

   Two things I learned are ...

   _____

   _____

2. Suppose there was another reading in this unit. Would you expect it to be about damage caused by earthquakes or hurricanes? Why?

   I would expect the next article in this ~~selection~~ unit to be about damaged caused by _____ because...

   _____

The Solar System

Earth is part of the solar system.

Where Do You Live?

You live in a home. Your home is on a street. Your street is in a town or a city. Your[25] town or city is in a state. Your state is in the United States.

You live on a planet, too. Your home that is on[50] a street in a town in a state in the United States is on the planet called Earth. Planet Earth is part of the solar[75] system.

The solar system is made up of the Sun and the many things that move around the Sun. We all live on planet Earth.[100] Earth is one of the nine planets that are part of this solar system.[114]

The Solar System

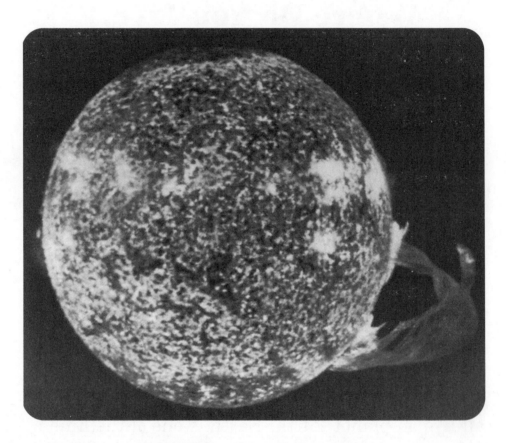

Hot gas shoots out from the Sun.

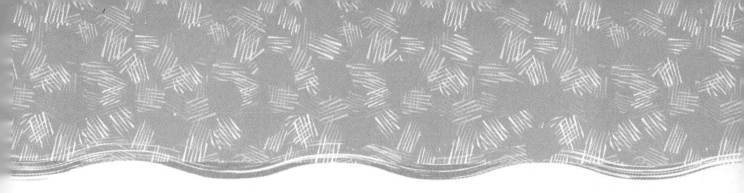

The Sun

When you look up into the sky on a clear night, you see lots of stars. Most of these stars are too far[25] away to see in the daytime. Yet you can see one star during the daytime—the Sun. The Sun is a very big star. It[50] is much bigger than any of the nine planets in its solar system.

Like all stars, the Sun is a big ball of gas that[75] spins around. This gas is very hot. Jets of hot gas shoot out from the Sun. The Sun's hot gas sends light and heat to[100] all of the planets. Earth would not have daylight without the Sun.[112]

The Solar System

This is how Mars looks from space.

Planets Close to the Sun

Planets that are close to the Sun get more heat and light than planets that are farther away from the Sun. Two planets in the solar system are closer to the Sun than Earth is. On these two planets, it can get as hot as 896 degrees. That is almost seven times hotter than it ever gets on Earth. The hottest it has been on Earth is 131 degrees.

The fourth planet from the Sun is Mars. Because Mars isn't as close to the Sun as Earth is, Mars doesn't get as hot as Earth does. The hottest it gets on Mars is 77 degrees.

The Solar System

The nine planets of our solar system move around
the Sun. Earth is the third planet from the Sun.

Far, Far Away

Five planets in the solar system lie beyond the planet Mars. All but one of these planets is much bigger than Earth.[25] Pluto is the smallest of all nine planets in the solar system. Pluto is also the planet farthest from the Sun.

The five planets that[50] are very far from the Sun do not get very much heat. It gets very cold on these planets. The coldest it has ever been[75] on Earth is −94 degrees. On Pluto it never gets warmer than −382 degrees. A warm day on Pluto is more than three times colder[100] than the coldest day on the coldest part of Earth![110]

The Solar System

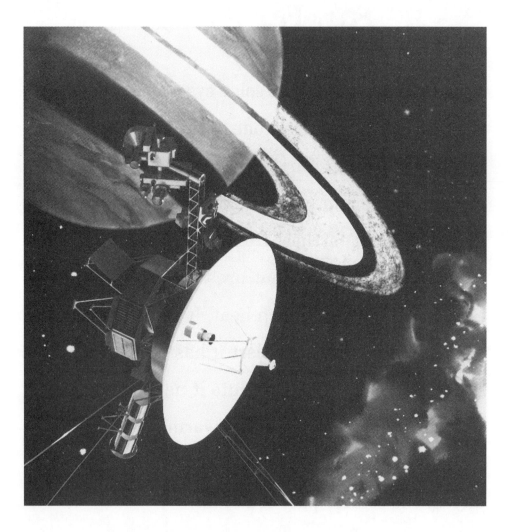

Telescopes on spaceships help people
learn about the solar system.

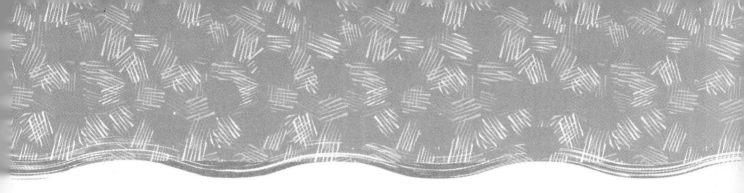

Learning About the Solar System

For hundreds of years, looking through a telescope was the only way people could learn about the solar system. When[25] things are far away, they look smaller. A telescope is a huge glass that makes things that are far away look bigger. Telescopes helped people[50] learn about the planets in the solar system and the stars in the sky.

With spaceships, people have learned much more about the solar system.[75] Some spaceships have carried people. A few spaceships that carry people have landed on the moon. Yet most spaceships carry cameras, not people. These cameras[100] take pictures that teach us more about our solar system.[110]

The Solar System

Write words that will help you remember what you learned.

Where Do You Live?

_____

_____

_____

_____

The Sun

_____

_____

_____

_____

Planets Close to the Sun

_____

_____

_____

_____

Far, Far Away

_____

_____

_____

_____

Learning About the Solar System

_____

_____

_____

_____

Where Do You Live?

1. "Where Do You Live?" is MAINLY about _____

    Ⓐ how to use a map.

    Ⓑ where you are in the solar system.

    Ⓒ the planet Earth.

    Ⓓ where the United States is.

2. What is the solar system?

_____

_____

_____

The Sun

1. What is a star?

    Ⓐ It is a planet.

    Ⓑ It is the solar system.

    Ⓒ It is the sky.

    Ⓓ It is a big ball of gas.

2. What is the Sun?

_____

_____

_____

Planets Close to the Sun

1. Why is Earth hotter than Mars?

   Ⓐ Earth is far from Mars.

   Ⓑ Mars is far from the solar system.

   Ⓒ Earth is closer to the Sun than Mars.

   Ⓓ Earth is farther from the Sun than Mars.

2. How are the planets that are closer to the Sun different from the planets that are farther away from the Sun?

_____

_____

_____

Far, Far Away

1. Another good name for "Far, Far Away" is ____

   Ⓐ "Planets Far From the Sun."

   Ⓑ "Planets in Far Away Solar Systems."

   Ⓒ "Pluto, the Warmest Planet."

   Ⓓ "Earth and Pluto."

2. Describe the planets that are beyond Mars.

_____

_____

_____

Learning About the Solar System

1. The main idea of "Learning About the Solar System" is _____

Ⓐ there are several ways to learn about the solar system.

Ⓑ you need a spaceship to get to the moon.

Ⓒ no one uses telescopes now.

Ⓓ cameras can teach us about the solar system.

2. What are two ways to learn about the solar system?

_____

_____

_____

Connect Your Ideas

1. What do you think the two most important things are to know about the solar system?

_____

_____

_____

2. Which planet would you like to visit? Why?

_____

_____

_____

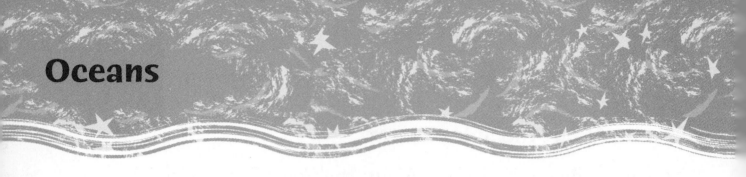

Oceans

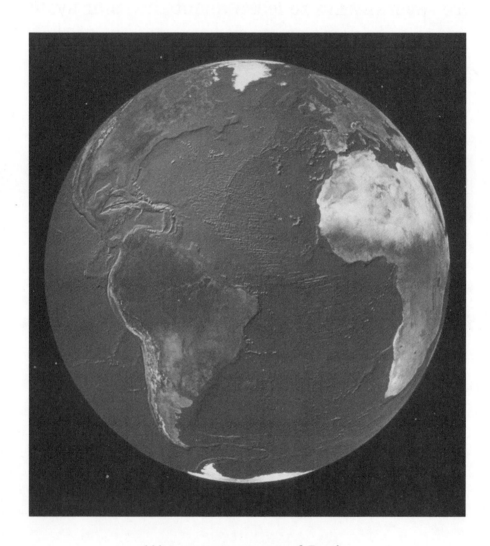

Water covers most of Earth.
The dark parts of the picture are water.

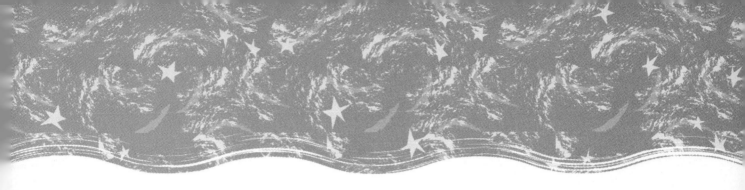

The Ocean

As you read this, you are on land. Yet if you were out in space looking at Earth, you would see more water[25] than land. Water covers almost 75% of Earth. Most of this water is in four oceans. The oceans are joined together. The oceans are really[50] one big mass of water.

The big land masses that rise above the oceans are called continents. There are seven continents. Land masses that are[75] smaller than continents are called islands. Earth has many islands. Oceans and land masses are different in many ways. Yet they are the same in[100] one way. Under both the oceans and the continents are rocks.[111]

The ocean floor has deep valleys like the land does.

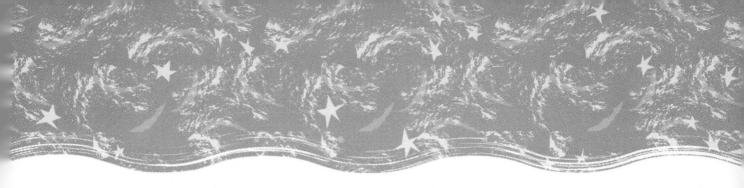

The Ocean Floor

Maps make it look like the ocean is smooth. Yet the ocean floor is just like the land. It has mountains, valleys,[25] and plains. The tallest mountain on Earth is on the ocean floor. The ocean floor also has deep valleys and large plains.

At the edge[50] of a continent, the land slopes into the ocean. This slope of land is called the continental shelf. The ocean is not very deep along[75] the continental shelf. However, the continental shelf ends in a steep cliff. At the edge of the cliff, the ocean is very deep. The deepest[100] part of the ocean is about seven miles below the land.[111]

Many kinds of plants and animals live on coral reefs.

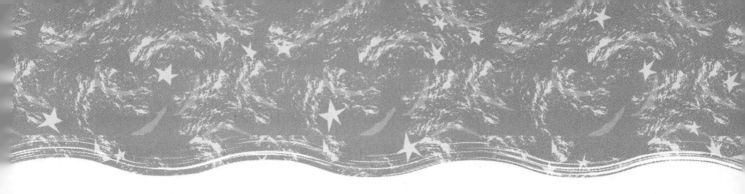

Coral Reefs

The ocean has many layers. Different animals and plants live in these different layers. In some warm places, little animals called corals live [25] in the top layer of the ocean. Each coral is the size of the tip of a pen. Corals live side by side and do [50] not move. When corals die, their hard shells stick together. New corals grow on top of the old shells.

Over a long time, a pile [75] of coral shells can grow very high. This pile of shells is called a coral reef. Some coral reefs look like large bushes growing in [100] the ocean. Coral reefs make good homes for many ocean animals and plants. [113]

Oceans

Waves crash against the coast.

Coasts

The winds that blow over the ocean make waves. These waves are moving all the time. When the waves get to the land, they[25] crash against the land. The land that the ocean hits is called a coast.

In some places, the land on the coast is made up[50] of high cliffs. If the land on the coast is low, the waves break the rocks on the land into small stones. Over a long[75] time, the small stones get smaller and smaller. The small stones become sand. After many years, the low land becomes a beach with lots of[100] sand. These sandy beaches can be good places on which to play.[112]

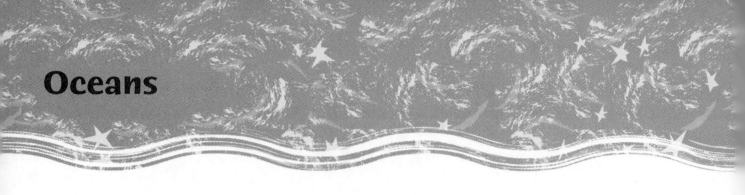

Oceans

Ocean storms can bring strong winds and rain to land.

Oceans and Weather

The weather of the land near the ocean is closely linked to the ocean. Water gets hot and cold more slowly than [25] land does. Once the ocean's water is warm, it stays warm. That is why places close to the coast are warmer in winter than places [50] inland. Yet once the ocean gets cool, it stays cool. Cool winds blow toward the land during the summer even when it is hot inland. [75] This is why summers may be cool on the coast when other places are hot.

Earth's oceans also have an effect on storms. Many storms [100] start over the ocean. Storms can bring strong winds and rain to land. [113]

Write words that will help you remember what you learned.

The Ocean

_____

_____

_____

_____

The Ocean Floor

_____

_____

_____

_____

Coral Reefs

_____

_____

_____

_____

Coasts

_____

_____

_____

_____

Oceans and Weather

_____

_____

_____

_____

The Ocean

1. Another good name for "The Ocean" is ⎯⎯

Ⓐ "Oceans in Space."

Ⓑ "The Continents."

Ⓒ "Water on Earth."

Ⓓ "Land Masses."

2. Describe the way Earth looks from space.

_____

_____

_____

The Ocean Floor

1. The main idea of "The Ocean Floor" is that ⎯⎯

Ⓐ the ocean floor is smooth like the water.

Ⓑ the ocean floor has mountains like the land.

Ⓒ the ocean floor is very rocky.

Ⓓ the ocean floor is very deep.

2. Describe how the ocean floor looks.

_____

_____

_____

Coral Reefs

1. Where do corals live?

Ⓐ in the top layer of the ocean

Ⓑ on sea plants

Ⓒ in the deep part of the ocean

Ⓓ floating in the ocean

2. How do coral reefs form?

_____

_____

_____

Coasts

1. What is the most important idea in "Coasts"?

Ⓐ Waves crash against land.

Ⓑ Waves form sand.

Ⓒ The coast is where the waves hit the land.

Ⓓ The coast is always windy.

2. How is sand made?

_____

_____

_____

Oceans and Weather

1. "Oceans and Weather" is MAINLY about _____

   Ⓐ why the ocean is warm in the summer and the winter.

   Ⓑ how storms start over the ocean.

   Ⓒ why the ocean has waves.

   Ⓓ how the weather on the ocean changes the weather on the land.

2. How are the oceans and weather linked?

   _____

   _____

   _____

Connect Your Ideas

1. What are two ways that the oceans are linked to the land?

   _____

   _____

   _____

2. Suppose there was another reading in this unit. Would you expect it to be about fish or about cats? Why?

   _____

   _____

   _____

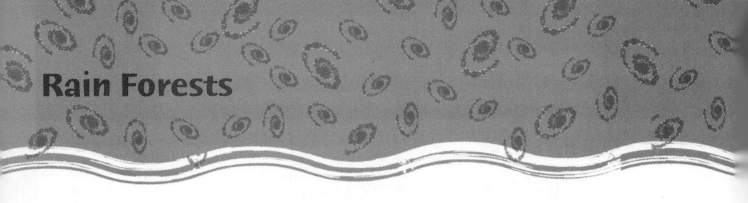

Rain forests have many tall trees.

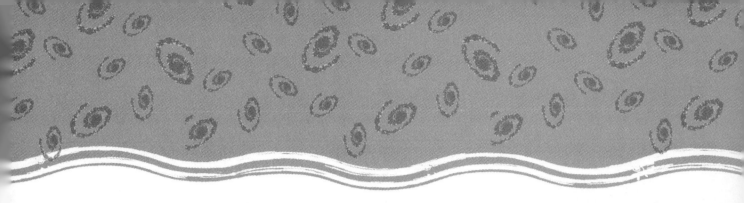

What Is a Rain Forest?

In places where it rains and rains, many different kinds of plants and trees grow. Many animals live among these[25] plants and trees. These places are called rain forests. The biggest rain forest is near the Amazon River in South America. It is hot and[50] rainy there for most of the year.

In the rain forest near the Amazon River, tall trees grow close to one another. The leaves of[75] these tall trees are like a roof for the plants under them. Rain may not hit the smaller plants. Instead, the smaller plants get water[100] that runs down the trees or falls from the leaves of the trees.[113]

Rain Forests

This animal is trying to hide from the rain in a rain forest.

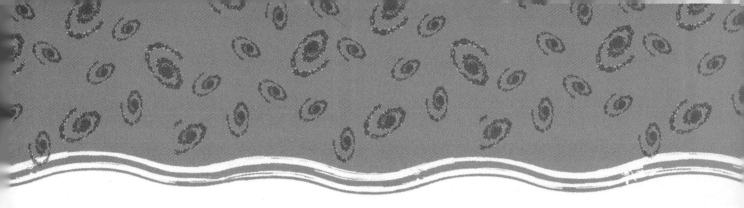

How Much Rain Falls?

Rain falls for much of the year in the rain forest. The Amazon rain forest can get up to 10 feet[25] of rain each year. Some years, it gets much more rain. How tall is 10 feet? The walls of most rooms are eight feet tall.[50] So a pail would need to be higher than the walls of a room to catch 10 feet of rain.

Some places in the United[75] States, such as parts of Florida, can get a lot of rain. These places in Florida can get five feet of rain each year. The[100] Amazon rain forest gets twice as much rain as Florida does.[111]

An orchid mantis hides on an orchid flower.

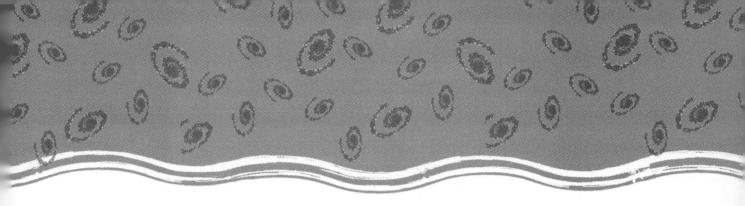

The Orchid Plant
and Insect

There are many unusual plants in the Amazon rain forest. One unusual plant is the orchid. Orchids have some of the most beautiful flowers on earth. Orchids grow in many shapes and colors. Orchids have strong smells to bring insects to them. Insects spread pollen among orchids. This pollen helps the orchids grow.

One insect does not need a strong smell to come to orchids. This insect is called the orchid mantis. The orchid mantis looks just like the flower of an orchid. The orchid mantis hides among the flowers of orchids. It then catches other insects that stop on orchid flowers close to it.

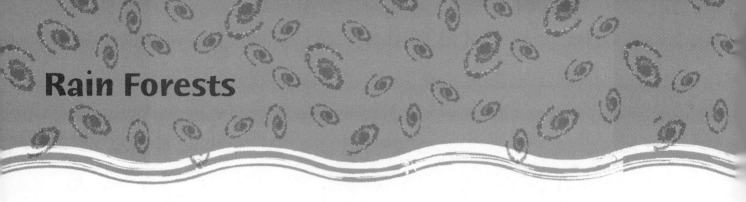

The toucan's bill has many bright colors.

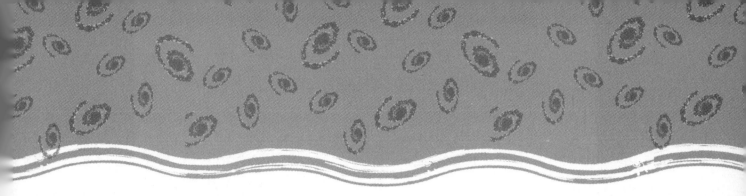

The Toucan's Bill

One kind of bird that lives in the rain forest is the parrot. Parrots have green, yellow, and red feathers. Another bird[25] has many colors, too. This bird is the toucan. You would not see all of the toucan's colors if you just looked at its feathers[50]. The toucan's feathers are black and white with small yellow or red spots.

The toucan's other colors are on its bill. The toucan's bill is[75] very big and brightly colored. Scientists think that the size of the toucan's bill helps keep the toucan safe from other birds. The bright colors[100] of the toucan's bill also help toucans find each other in the rain forest.[114]

Many kinds of animals and plants live in rain forests.

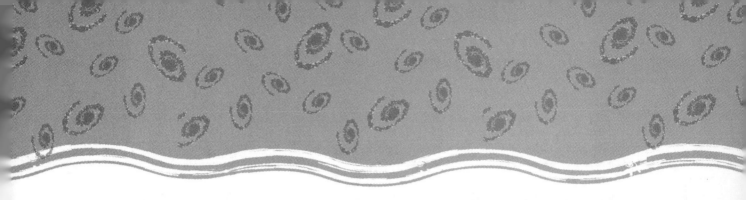

Why Are Rain Forests Important?

Rain forests are important to people, other animals, and plants. Rain forests cover only a small part of the earth.[25] However, they are home to half of all the animals and plants on earth.

Many things people need come from rain forests. Some plants help[50] sick people get well.

Foods like oranges and nuts grow in rain forests. The sap from rubber trees is made into rubber. Rubber is used[75] to make things we use every day, like balls and tires.

Rain forests keep weather the same in many parts of the world. When trees[100] are cut down in rain forests, weather can change all over the world.[113]

Rain Forests

Write words that will help you remember what you learned.

What Is a Rain Forest?

_____

_____

_____

_____

How Much Rain Falls?

_____

_____

_____

_____

The Orchid Plant and Insect

_____

_____

_____

_____

The Toucan's Bill

_____

_____

_____

_____

Why Are Rain Forests Important?

_____

_____

_____

_____

What Is a Rain Forest?

1. What is the Amazon rain forest like?

Ⓐ Many animals but not many plants live there.

Ⓑ It is cold and rainy.

Ⓒ It is hot and rainy.

Ⓓ Many plants but not many animals live there.

2. What is a rain forest?

_____

_____

_____

How Much Rain Falls?

1. What is another name for "How Much Rain Falls?"

Ⓐ "The Amazon Rain Forest"

Ⓑ "Rain in Florida"

Ⓒ "The Wet, Wet Rain Forest"

Ⓓ "Rain Forests in Florida"

2. Does the Amazon rain forest or Florida get more rain each year? Explain.

_____

_____

_____

Rain Forests

The Orchid Plant and Insect

1. What is the main idea of "The Orchid Plant and Insect"?

Ⓐ There is an orchid plant and an insect that looks just like it.

Ⓑ The orchid plant is really an insect.

Ⓒ The orchid is an unusual plant.

Ⓓ The orchid mantis smells like an orchid.

2. How do insects help orchids?

_____

_____

_____

The Toucan's Bill

1. How is a toucan like a parrot?

Ⓐ Both have colorful beaks.

Ⓑ Both have black and white feathers with small orange spots.

Ⓒ Both have many different colors.

Ⓓ Both have many kinds of feathers.

2. Why is the toucan's bill special?

_____

_____

_____

Why Are Rain Forests Important?

1. Another good name for "Why Are Rain Forests Important?" is _____

Ⓐ "Why People Need the Rain Forest."

Ⓑ "Animals in the Rain Forest."

Ⓒ "Plants from the Rain Forest."

Ⓓ "Foods from the Rain Forest."

2. Why is the rain forest important?

_____

_____

_____

Connect Your Ideas

1. What do you think it would be like to live in the rain forest?

_____

_____

_____

2. Name two reasons rain forests are important.

_____

_____

_____

Economics

When you shop, you take part in economics.

What Is Economics?

You have probably gone shopping for food or clothes with your family. You might have been paid for feeding someone's cat or[25] for washing a car. Whenever you buy things like food or clothes or get paid for doing a job, you are taking part in economics.[50] Economics has to do with making, buying, and selling things that people want or need.

Economics started when people traded one thing for something else.[75] Today, people sometimes trade one thing for something else. They usually use money. When you buy something, you trade money for the thing you want.[100] When you get paid for a job, you trade your work for money.[113]

Economics

Many companies make things to sell
in stores. This company makes food.

Making Things

Economics starts with someone making things for people to buy. Usually, groups of people work together in a company to make things. A[25] company decides many things before it starts making something. For example, a bike company decides what size and color its bikes will be.

Next, people[50] need to be hired to make the bikes. A company needs money to pay these workers. The company also needs money to buy materials, such[75] as steel for the bike frame and rubber for the tires. Then, the workers have to shape the steel and rubber into the right parts.[100] Finally, the workers put the parts together to make bikes.[110]

Economics

Sales people can help people choose the right bike.

Selling Things

Many companies don't sell their bikes to people. They sell their bikes to stores. Then these stores sell the bikes to people.

Store [25] owners need to have money to pay a company for the bikes. Store owners also need a place to sell the bikes. They need sales [50] people to help people choose a bike. Store owners need to pay their sales people, too.

Store owners also need to set the price of [75] a bike. This price should be more than the store owner paid for it. Yet the bike should cost the same as or less than [100] bikes in other stores. After all, many people compare different stores' prices. [112]

Economics

Young people can earn money in many ways.

Making and Saving Money

Before people can buy things, they need money to pay for them. Most people make money by working. They save the[25] money they earn to buy the things they want.

By saving money in banks, people earn even more money. Saving money in banks works this[50] way. You get $20 for doing a job. You put that money into a savings account in a bank. The bank pays you so that[75] it can use your money. In a year, you will have almost $21 in your savings account. You will have earned $1 for keeping your[100] money in the bank. Making and saving money are also part of economics.[113]

Economics

Trading is another way to get something you want.

Being a Smart Shopper

Smart shoppers compare. For example, they may compare several bikes. They may study newspapers to find the best prices. They may [25] wait for sales. Smart shoppers decide how much money they will spend before they choose a bike.

Smart shoppers may decide to buy a cheaper [50] bike. Then they will have money left over to save or to buy something else. At other times, smart shoppers go to used-bike stores. [75] There they can buy bikes for lower prices.

Sometimes, smart shoppers also trade for what they want. They find someone who has what they want. [100] Then they trade something they have. Many people trade bikes, games, or cards. [113]

Economics

Write words that will help you remember what you learned.

What Is Economics?

_____

_____

_____

_____

Making Things

_____

_____

_____

_____

Selling Things

_____

_____

_____

_____

Making and Saving Money

_____

_____

_____

_____

Being a Smart Shopper

_____

_____

_____

_____

What Is Economics?

1. Another good name for "What Is Economics?" is _____

Ⓐ "Trading Money for Food and Clothes."

Ⓑ "Shopping Is Economics."

Ⓒ "Economics in Your Life."

Ⓓ "Trading Can Be Fun."

2. What is economics?

_____

_____

_____

Making Things

1. The most important idea in "Making Things" is _____

Ⓐ how companies make things to sell.

Ⓑ that people work in groups.

Ⓒ that companies need materials and workers.

Ⓓ how companies decide what they will make.

2. How does a company make things?

_____

_____

_____

Selling Things

1. Why does a store owner need money?

   Ⓐ to make bikes that people want to buy

   Ⓑ to buy bikes to sell and to pay sales people

   Ⓒ to sell bikes and to set prices for bikes

   Ⓓ to find bikes to sell to stores

2. Retell what you learned about selling things.

   _____

   _____

   _____

Making and Saving Money

1. Why do people save money?

   Ⓐ to earn money in a bank

   Ⓑ to have money to buy what they want

   Ⓒ to get a job

   Ⓓ to keep the money they earn

2. How can you earn money in a bank?

   _____

   _____

   _____

Being a Smart Shopper

1. Another good name for "Being a Smart Shopper" is _____

Ⓐ "Spending Money Wisely."

Ⓑ "Shopping at Stores that Sell Used Things."

Ⓒ "How to Find Sales."

Ⓓ "Spending What You Have Earned."

2. How can someone become a smart shopper?

_____

_____

_____

Connect Your Ideas

1. How is economics part of your life every day?

_____

_____

_____

2. Tell about a time you saved money to buy something.

_____

_____

_____

Reading Log · Level C · Book 2

	I Read This	New Words I Learned	New Facts I Learned	What Else I Want to Learn About This Subject
Hurricanes				
What Is a Hurricane?				
Tracking Hurricanes				
Hurricane Cleanup				
Pets in Hurricanes				
Hurricane Names				
Earthquakes				
What Is an Earthquake?				
Predicting and Measuring Earthquakes				
Duck, Cover, and Hold				
Underwater Earthquakes				
Old Stories About Earthquakes				
The Solar System				
Where Do You Live?				
The Sun				
Planets Close to the Sun				
Far, Far Away				
Learning About the Solar System				

	I Read This	New Words I Learned	New Facts I Learned	What Else I Want to Learn About This Subject
Oceans				
The Ocean				
The Ocean Floor				
Coral Reefs				
Coasts				
Oceans and Weather				
Rain Forests				
What Is a Rain Forest?				
How Much Rain Falls?				
The Orchid Plant and Insect				
The Toucan's Bill				
Why Are Rain Forests Important?				
Economics				
What Is Economics?				
Making Things				
Selling Things				
Making and Saving Money				
Being a Smart Shopper				

Self-Check Graph

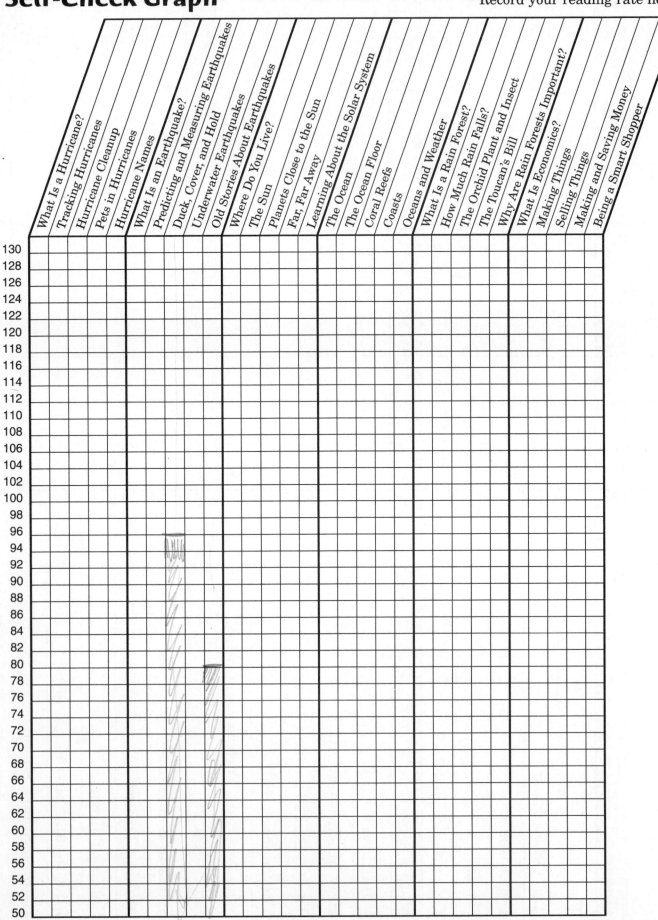

Column headers (diagonal):
What Is a Hurricane? · Tracking Hurricanes · Hurricane Cleanup · Pets in Hurricanes · Hurricane Names · What Is an Earthquake? · Predicting and Measuring Earthquakes · Duck, Cover, and Hold · Underwater Earthquakes · Old Stories About Earthquakes · Where Do You Live? · The Sun · Planets Close to the Sun · Far, Far Away · Learning About the Solar System · The Ocean · The Ocean Floor · Coral Reefs · Coasts · Oceans and Weather · What Is a Rain Forest? · How Much Rain Falls? · The Orchid Plant and Insect · The Toucan's Bill · Why Are Rain Forests Important? · What Is Economics? · Making Things · Selling Things · Making and Saving Money · Being a Smart Shopper

Vertical scale: 130, 128, 126, 124, 122, 120, 118, 116, 114, 112, 110, 108, 106, 104, 102, 100, 98, 96, 94, 92, 90, 88, 86, 84, 82, 80, 78, 76, 74, 72, 70, 68, 66, 64, 62, 60, 58, 56, 54, 52, 50